The Union Victory
(July 1863–1865)

Dale Anderson

WORLD ALMANAC® LIBRARY

Please visit our web site at: www.worldalmanaclibrary.com
For a free color catalog describing World Almanac® Library's
list of high-quality books and multimedia programs,
call 1-800-848-2928 (USA) or 1-800-387-3178 (Canada).
World Almanac® Library's fax: (414) 332-3567.

Library of Congress Cataloging-in-Publication Data

Anderson, Dale, 1953-
    The Union victory: (July 1863-1865) / by Dale Anderson.
        p. cm. — (World Almanac Library of the Civil War)
    Includes bibliographical references and index.
    ISBN 0-8368-5584-1 (lib. bdg.)
    ISBN 0-8368-5593-0 (softcover)
    1. United States—History—Civil War, 1861-1865—
Campaigns—Juvenile literature. [1. United States—History—
Civil War, 1861-1865—Campaigns.] I. Title. II. Series.
    E470.A53 2004
    973.7'3—dc22   2003062489

First published in 2004 by
World Almanac® Library
330 West Olive Street, Suite 100
Milwaukee, WI 53212 USA

Copyright © 2004 by World Almanac® Library.

Produced by Discovery Books
Project editor: Geoff Barker
Editors: Betsy Rasmussen and Valerie J. Weber
Designer and page production: Laurie Shock, Shock Design, Inc.
Photo researcher: Rachel Tisdale
Consultant: Andrew Frank, Assistant Professor of History, Florida
    Atlantic University
Maps: Stefan Chabluk
World Almanac® editorial direction: Mark Sachner
World Almanac® art direction: Tammy Gruenewald

Photo credits: Peter Newark's American Pictures: cover, pp. 6, 8, 11, 13,
19 (top), 20, 22, 23 (right), 24, 28, 30, 35 (top), 36, 39, 41, 42, 43
(right); Library of Congress: pp. 7, 15, 27, 31, 32, 38; Corbis: pp. 9, 12,
17, 18, 19 (bottom), 25, 26, 29 (both), 34, 40, 43 (left).

Printed in the United States of America

1 2 3 4 5 6 7 8 9 08 07 06 05 04

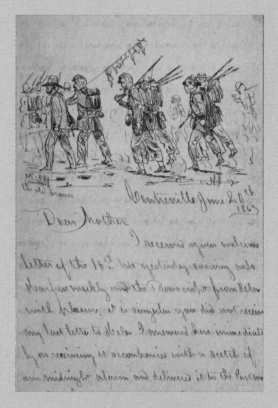

*"To my mother, who got me
Bruce Catton; my brother,
who shared my passion for the
Civil War; and my wife and
sons, who cheerfully put up
with several field trips and
countless anecdotes."*

— DALE ANDERSON

Cover: General Robert E. Lee (*seated, left*) signs
an agreement surrendering his Confederate army
in Virginia in April 1865 as Union general
Ulysses S. Grant (*seated, right*) looks on.

Contents

While the Confederate states covered about as much territory as the Union states, they held fewer people, fewer factories, and fewer railroad tracks and locomotives. These would be significant drawbacks for the Confederacy during the Civil War. The South would also lose part of its support when West Virginia separated from the rest of Virginia in 1863.

The War between the States

The Civil War was fought between 1861 and 1865. It was the bloodiest conflict in United States history, with more soldiers killed and wounded than in any other war. It was also a pivotal event in U.S. history: It transformed the lives of millions of African-American men, women, and children by freeing them from slavery. It also transformed the nation, changing it from a loose confederation of states into a powerful country with a strong central government.

On one side were eleven southern states that had split from the United States to form a new country, the Confederate States of America, led by President Jefferson Davis. They took this step after Abraham Lincoln was elected president of the United

States in 1860. Southerners feared Lincoln would end slavery, which was central to their economy and society. The northern states, or the **Union**, declared this split illegal.

A big question was whether the four **Border States** (Delaware, Maryland, Kentucky, and Missouri) would join the **Confederacy**. They had slavery, too, but they also held many people loyal to the Union. To keep control of these states, Lincoln felt early in the war that he could not risk moving against slavery, fearing that to do so would drive the Border States out of the Union. Later, however, he did declare the emancipation, or freedom, of Southern slaves.

In the Border States, and in many others, families divided sharply, with some men fighting for one side and some for the other. The Civil War has been called a war of "brother against brother."

Fighting broke out on April 12, 1861, when gunners for the South began shelling Union soldiers in Fort Sumter in Charleston Harbor, South Carolina. This attack led Lincoln to call for troops to put down what he called an armed rebellion. Thousands of Northerners flocked to the Union army. Thousands of Southerners joined the Confederate army, determined to win independence for their side.

Soldiers in both the Union and Confederate armies suffered the hardships—and occasional boredom—of life in an army camp. They also fought in huge battles with great bravery and heroism. At times, both sides treated their enemies with honor and respect. At other times, they treated them with cruelty and brutality.

The opposing armies fought in two main areas, or theaters. The eastern theater included Virginia, Maryland, and Pennsylvania; the region near the Confederate capital of Richmond, Virginia; and the Union capital of Washington, D.C. The huge western theater stretched from eastern Kentucky and Tennessee down to the Gulf of Mexico and all the way to New Mexico.

From 1861 to 1863 in the East, Confederate general Robert E. Lee beat back several attempts by Northern armies to capture Richmond. Twice he boldly invaded the North, hoping that stunning victories would persuade Britain and France to recognize the independence of the South and give it vital aid. Both invasions, however, ended.

In the West, the Union army saw more success up to 1863. It gained control of both the Mississippi River, an important transportation route, and the Confederate state of Tennessee.

CHAPTER ONE

Up to the Heights

The losses at Gettysburg and Vicksburg left
many in the South despairing:

*"Events have succeeded one another with disas-
trous rapidity. One brief month ago we were apparently
at the point of success. . . . Now the picture is just as
somber as it was bright then. . . . The Confederacy
totters to its destruction."*

William Gorgas, a Confederate general, July 28, 1863

The Summer of 1863

Both the eastern and the western
theaters saw major Union victories in
July 1863. In the East, Robert E. Lee's
Confederate army suffered a bitter
defeat in the three-day battle fought at
Gettysburg, Pennsylvania. In the West,
Union general Ulysses S. Grant finally
forced the surrender of Southern
troops at Vicksburg, Mississippi. This
gave the North control of the
Mississippi River, a vital route for
transporting supplies and troops.

These losses had political conse-
quences. In late June, Confederate
president Jefferson Davis had author-
ized Vice President Alexander
Stephens to travel to Washington,

Union soldiers and officers were better clothed,
armed, and supplied than their Confederate
counterparts, an advantage that would prove
important in the last years of the war.

D.C., to suggest peace terms to Abraham Lincoln. When news of Gettysburg arrived, however, Lincoln refused to even meet with Stephens. In addition, the British government had considered recognizing the independence of the South and possibly providing badly needed aid, but the twin defeats convinced it not to take that action.

All Quiet on the Eastern Front

The eastern theater saw little action in late 1863. Lee's Confederate army licked its wounds in Virginia, while Union general George Meade was reluctant to attack. In late November, Meade finally moved south, but Lee maneuvered into a new position to block him. Soon after, the two eastern armies retired to winter quarters.

In the fall and winter of 1863, attention shifted to the fighting in eastern Tennessee, which was so important that some troops were pulled from the

Alexander Stephens wanted to persuade old friend Abraham Lincoln to accept peace. He and President Davis hoped that a Lee victory in the North in the summer of 1863 would strengthen his argument.

eastern armies and sent west. Lee sent General James Longstreet's **corps** to reinforce Confederates in Tennessee, and two corps were later sent from Meade's army to help Union troops there.

Chattanooga Lost

In September of 1863, General William Rosecrans led the Union Army of the Cumberland into southeastern Tennessee. Rosecrans forced Confederate general Braxton Bragg's Army of the Tennessee to abandon Chattanooga, a terrible loss to the South because the city was a vital rail center, key to bringing supplies and troops to the front. "We are now in the darkest hour of our political existence," Jefferson Davis wrote gloomily.

By the middle of September, Bragg had received some **reinforcements**, including the first of Longstreet's troops. He decided to hit the Union army, now camped in northwestern Georgia, along Chickamauga Creek.

A Confederate soldier later recalled a "solid, unbroken wave of awe-inspiring sound" from the heavy fighting at Chickamauga.

Chickamauga

On September 19, 1863, Bragg threw his troops at the left side of the Union line, where General George Thomas commanded a corps. All day long, the fighting raged. Finally, the two sides rested for the night.

That night, General James Longstreet and the rest of his Confederate troops arrived. Bragg was determined to strike again with the fresh soldiers. The next day, Longstreet's men were lucky; they attacked an area where Rosecrans happened to be without Union soldiers. The Confederates stormed through the gap and quickly turned on the Northern troops on either side of it. Soon nearly one-third of Rosecrans's army—including its commander—was fleeing back to Chattanooga.

Longstreet's troops then swung around to attack Thomas's corps. Although they were outnumbered and the fighting was fierce, Thomas's men held firm. Union **reserves** arrived just in time to stop a breakthrough. The Union forces beat back the Confederates, who finally pulled back. That night, Thomas's men retreated to Chattanooga.

Chickamauga was the biggest—and bloodiest—battle in the West. Rosecrans had nearly 16,200 Union **casualties**, while Bragg lost nearly 18,500 Confederates. After the battle, Bragg's corps commanders urged him to attack Chattanooga; the Union army, they said, was in a panic. When Bragg refused to do so immediately, Rosecrans had time to regroup.

Chattanooga

Rosecrans soon found himself in a trap. Bragg decided his army had recovered from Chickamauga and moved them to Chattanooga. He positioned his army on the high ground south of the city, bottling up the Union army. Since only a trickle of supplies could get past the Confederates, the Northern troops were getting hungry.

Union forces moved quickly to help, sending two corps to Tennessee. William Tecumseh Sherman was also sent with reinforcements from Grant's army on the Mississippi. In October, Grant—now Union commander of the entire western theater—arrived in Chattanooga. Union troops carried out a plan to break the stranglehold on

GEORGE THOMAS

*George Thomas was born in Virginia in 1816 and graduated from **West Point** in 1840. Known as a good **artillery** officer, he taught that subject at West Point before the war.*

*Thomas chose to remain in the U.S. Army when the war broke out, even after Virginia **seceded**. He fought at Perryville and Stones River and won the nickname the "Rock of Chickamauga" for his stand at that battle. He was later placed in command of the Army of the Cumberland. After the war, he was stationed for duty in California, where he died in 1870.*

supplies. This move opened a route called "the cracker line" because it was used to bring in badly needed food.

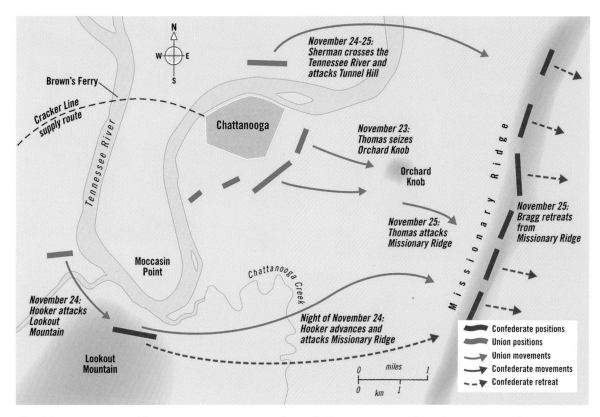

The Union army in Chattanooga was trapped until Grant approved a plan to seize key crossing points west of the city. This opened the "cracker line" to supply the Union army.

TROUBLE AT THE TOP

After Chickamauga, Confederate president Jefferson Davis visited Bragg's army. There, four corps commanders told him—in front of Bragg—to remove the general from command. Feeling he had no replacement, however, Davis left Bragg in charge. He even urged him to split his army, sending Longstreet to attack Union forces in Kentucky. With these two decisions, Davis invited disaster.

Unhappy with Rosecrans's performance at Chickamauga and Chattanooga, Grant also replaced him with Thomas as commander of the Union's Army of the Cumberland.

Grant next looked for a way to oust Bragg's forces. In late November, he launched his attacks. On November 23 and 24, 1863, Union troops gained the high-ground positions of Orchard Knob and Lookout Mountain, which left Bragg's main force on Missionary Ridge.

On November 25, Grant attacked the ridge. When Sherman

Union forces attack Confederates on Lookout Mountain. The assault took place in heavy fog, which led some observers to call this fight the "Battle above the Clouds."

became bogged down on the eastern side of the ridge, Grant unleashed Thomas's Army of the Cumberland against the Confederates at the base of the western part. Thomas's army quickly overran the Southern positions there. Then—though they had no orders to do so—they kept going. Determined to recover their pride after the defeat at Chickamauga, they slogged up the slope. As one Union officer reported, "Officers and men alike vied with each other in deeds of gallantry and bravery, cheering one another on to the goal for which we were contending."

The attack sent the Confederates flying. Bragg finally regrouped his soldiers 30 miles (50 kilometers) to the south. An appalled Bragg said there was "no satisfactory excuse for the shameful conduct of our troops." At last, Davis recognized that he could not leave Bragg in command and put Joseph Johnston in his place as commander of the Army of the Tennessee.

CHAPTER TWO

Grant Takes Command

Eighty-six men from Company I of the Fifty-seventh Massachusetts went into the Battle of the Wilderness in 1864. These nine were the only ones left uninjured after the battle.

Lincoln Finds His General

With victories at Vicksburg and Chattanooga, Grant was the North's new military hero. In February 1864, Congress created the post of lieutenant general—the highest rank in the army. Lincoln quickly named Grant to that rank and gave him command of all Union armies. Grant then put Sherman in command in the West. Henry Halleck, who had been commander of all the Union armies, was moved to a lower job, becoming chief of staff, an administrative position in the army.

Grant devised a simple and very aggressive strategy. Meade would attack Lee. Sherman would attack Johnston. Other smaller Union armies would attack the Confederates they faced. Everyone would move at the same time.

Interestingly, Lincoln had considered this very idea two years earlier. In January of 1862, he had suggested to Henry Halleck that the Union should "menac[e] [the Confederacy] with superior forces at *different* points, at the *same* time." Halleck had rejected the idea then. Now Lincoln had a general who shared his vision.

The Eastern Armies

After spending time in their winter quarters, the Union Army of the Potomac was ready to move. General Meade had nearly 120,000 men compared to only 62,000 or so for General Lee. The Confederates were confident, however, as one soldier revealed in a letter to his wife: "Lee's army is now the great hope of the South. The army here thinks it can whip its weight in wild cats and has no mistrusts or apprehension." Grant found the Union army equally confident. He wrote to Halleck, "The Army of the Potomac is in splendid condition and evidently feels like whipping somebody."

EDWIN STANTON

For most of the Civil War, Lincoln's Secretary of War was Edwin Stanton. Born in 1814 in Ohio, Stanton became a lawyer. When the Civil War began, he wholeheartedly backed Lincoln's decision to try to preserve the Union and served as legal advisor to Lincoln's first secretary of war, Simon Cameron. When Cameron was forced to resign while being investigated for dishonesty, Stanton replaced him.

Stanton was a tireless worker and an efficient organizer. Scrupulously honest, he ended the widespread corruption under Cameron and made sure that the Union armies received high-quality equipment and supplies. After the war, Stanton clashed with Lincoln's successor as president, Andrew Johnson, over how to treat the defeated South. Johnson finally fired him. Stanton died in 1869.

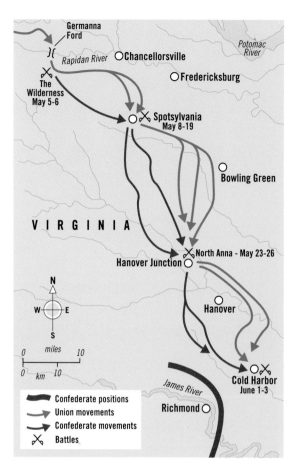

In the spring and early summer of 1864, Grant kept moving to his left, hoping to get around Lee's army. Each time, Lee moved his army just as quickly and took up defensive positions to block Grant's advance.

Horrors in the Wilderness

In the spring of 1864, the Army of the Potomac moved south. It crossed the Rapidan River and reached the area near Chancellorsville, Virginia, where it had fought Lee the year before. This area was called the Wilderness because the woods were dense and tangled, making it difficult for **infantry** to move. While the woods slowed the Union army's progress, Lee struck.

On May 5 and 6, the two armies mauled each other in heavy fighting. The casualties from the two days of fighting were high for both sides, but they were particularly damaging to the Union—more than 17,500 Northerners compared to 7,750 of Lee's men. Forest fires, ignited by sparks from the gunfire, raced through the dry woods, burning some of the wounded and increasing their suffering.

Moving On

In the past, Union commanders in the East would have stayed put or retreated after such a battle. Grant was different. On May 7, he ordered the army to move south and east, hoping to get around behind Lee's army. Seeing that the army would not retreat, one Union veteran recalled, "Our spirits rose."

The two armies met again about 15 miles (25 km) southeast of Chancellorsville, near Spotsylvania Court House. Twice the Union army used huge masses of troops—twelve **regiments** one day and an entire corps the next—trying to break Lee's defensive line. On May 12, the Union attack was so powerful that the fate of Lee's army hung in the balance. One Union officer commented, "It seemed

This painting matches a Union officer's description of the fighting at Spotsylvania. The officer wrote, "It was chiefly a savage hand-to-hand fight across the breastworks. Rank after rank was riddled by shot and shell and bayonet thrust . . . then fresh troops rushed madly forward to replace the dead; and so the murderous work went on."

impossible that troops could stand so severe a fire." When Lee came to the front lines to organize the defense, his soldiers forced him to go to the rear so that his life would not be in danger; they then rallied to stop the advance of the Union army.

Once again, Grant took heavy losses—much heavier than Lee's. Realizing that he could not defeat

Lee's army at this time, he pulled out and moved east and south again.

Cold Harbor

The two armies confronted each other again in early June 1864, at Cold Harbor, Virginia. Once more, Grant threw masses of troops at Confederate lines. Once more, Lee's army beat them back. On June 3, in less than an hour,

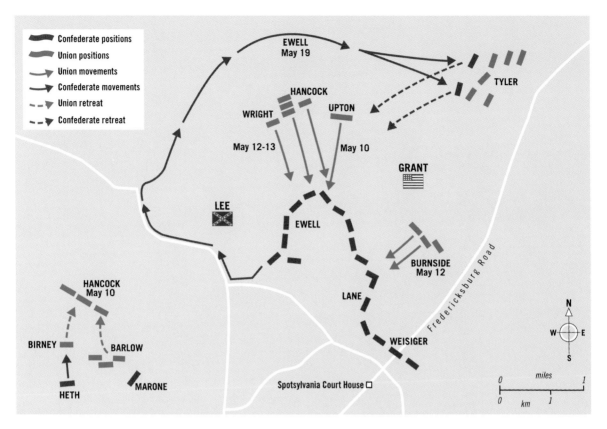

Hancock's May 12 attack on the "Bloody Angle" at Spotsylvania produced fighting that lasted from dawn until midnight, when Lee's troops pulled back to a new line.

the Union army suffered five thousand casualties, while the Confederate army suffered merely fifteen hundred casualties. The Northern soldiers had known the casualties would be heavy; before the attack, many soldiers grimly pinned their names to their uniforms so they could be identified if they died.

A Month of Casualties

From the Wilderness in early May to Cold Harbor a month later, the Union army suffered more than 40,000 casualties, while Lee's Confederates lost nearly 25,000. One Confederate described Grant as a general "who either does not know when he is whipped, or who cares not if he loses his whole Army." Grant simply did not accept that he was whipped; "I propose to fight it out on this line if it takes all summer," he wrote. Despite the Union's casualties, Grant knew that Lee's losses were bleeding his Confederate army and that the South was having a more difficult time finding soldiers to replace those lost in the many battles.

About Cold Harbor, Ulysses S. Grant later said, "I regret this assault more than any one I have ever ordered."

OFFENSE AND DEFENSE

The Union army's failure to take Lee's lines at Cold Harbor was yet another example of how defenders had the upper hand in the Civil War. Throughout the war, soldiers in well-entrenched positions generally beat back attacking forces. Unfortunately, generals who had studied the wars of the French emperor Napoleon continued to believe that the mass attacks that he had found successful would work.

*Another reason that Civil War generals favored attacks was the success that the U.S. Army had enjoyed in overrunning strong defensive positions in the Mexican War of 1846 to 1848. In many Civil War battles, however, the attacks came against tough veterans, not the untrained forces the U.S. soldiers had fought in Mexico. Those defenders hid in deep trenches fortified with **breastworks**, a tactic Napoleon had not contended with in his earlier wars. In addition, Civil War cannons, guns, and bullets were more deadly than those used in the Mexican War.*

Lee saw the danger he faced. He wrote: "We must destroy this army of Grant's before he gets to [the] James River. If he gets there, it will become a **siege**, and then it will be a mere question of time." Lee was right.

CHAPTER THREE

The Siege of Petersburg

~

Some Union soldiers paused during the long, dreary siege of Petersburg to have their picture taken.

The Plan for Petersburg

After the futile attack on Cold Harbor, Union commander Ulysses S. Grant decided to move again. His objective this time was Petersburg, Virginia, south of Richmond. Several rail lines reached Petersburg from the South, carrying vital supplies for Lee's army and for the Confederate capital. If Grant could get there first, he could cut off those supplies.

Grant's army moved secretly to Petersburg. The leading Union troops reached the area on June 15, 1864. They found 10 miles (16 km) of trenches and wooden breastworks 20 feet (6 meters) deep. Based on the experiences of the previous six weeks, the Union general on the scene refused to attack. He should have struck; only about twenty-five hundred Confederates were there. Within days, both armies were at Petersburg, with Lee's force strong enough to defend it.

Union forces could have taken the city earlier. General Benjamin Butler, leading nearly 30,000 troops, had been ordered by Grant to seize Petersburg in early May. Butler botched the job, however, and allowed a smaller Confederate force to trap him instead.

A Plan to Break the Siege

When the two armies settled in at Petersburg, a siege began. Grant tried various times to take Lee's lines but could do nothing to break through.

Grant's soldiers used mortars like this one to lob shells over the heads of Union troops to fall on the Confederates in their trenches.

BEN BUTLER

Benjamin Franklin Butler, born in New Hampshire in 1818, became a prominent lawyer and Democratic politician in Massachusetts before the war. He was one of several political generals, important politicians who were made officers to keep their support of the war.

Butler proved inept at command, though he made news. He was first to call runaway slaves **"contrabands** *of war." He won the nickname "Beast" Butler across the South by ordering that New Orleans women who insulted Union soldiers should be arrested as prostitutes. After Butler bungled two combat commands in 1864—and since his political support was no longer crucial to Lincoln—Grant fired him.*

After the war, Butler served in the House of Representatives and as governor of Massachusetts. In 1884, he ran for president but lost. He died in 1893.

In a siege, the attacking army tries to make the defending force surrender by keeping it cooped up and by cutting off its source of supplies. Typically, the attacking force also batters the defenders with artillery, hoping to both destroy defenses and weaken the enemy's will to fight.

Sieges can be very effective ways of winning key strongholds held by an enemy force. They can produce victory with little loss of life, and they typically lead to fewer casualties than a direct attack.

Sieges take time, however. The defensive force can hold out as long as it has food, water, and ammunition, and can reduce rations so that its soldiers can last longer. As sieges drag on with little happening, people on the home front might lose patience. They then often pressure the government— which, in turn, puts pressure on the attacking commander—to do something to end the siege.

A Union army colonel from Pennsylvania with a regiment full of coal miners had a clever idea. He suggested digging a tunnel beneath part of the Confederate line, blowing the fortifications up with gunpowder, and then attacking in strength. The plan was approved, and all through July, the troops tunneled. On July 30, 1864, it was time to attack.

The huge explosion buried an entire Confederate regiment in rubble. The attack failed, however. The blast created a huge crater; instead of moving around it, Northern soldiers flooded into it, becoming sitting ducks when the Confederates rallied. This "Battle of the Crater" cost the North about four thousand casualties—double those of the South.

The siege at Petersburg dragged on. For weeks, the two armies sat across from each other. Daily shelling made life miserable. The Confederates' supplies dwindled, but they hung on.

African-American troops bring cannons captured from the Confederates to Union lines during the siege at Petersburg.

Sherman Marches Toward Atlanta

During Confederate general Johnston's retreat to Atlanta, one Georgia soldier wrote to his wife:

"The truth is, we have run until I am getting out of heart [and] we must make a stand soon or the army will be demoralized."

Grant's Plan

In May 1864, as Grant moved against Lee in the East, William Tecumseh Sherman attacked with his 100,000-man Union army in the West. Facing him was Joseph Johnston's 62,000-strong Army of the Tennessee. Grant wanted Sherman to destroy Johnston's army and damage the Confederate countryside, so that the Southern army could no longer use its crops and farm animals to feed and transport its troops. Sherman moved south, aiming for Atlanta, Georgia, the Confederacy's most important rail center and a center for manufacturing arms and ammunition.

Johnston believed he could not defeat the Northerners in open battle and hoped to isolate small pieces of Sherman's force, then destroy them one at a time. Sherman managed to avoid this danger by maneuvering his forces in a brilliant manner, using some to hold Johnston in place while the rest marched around the Confederate army to a point farther south, thus forcing Johnston to pull back and enabling the rest of Sherman's force to join the leader. Repeating the maneuver, Sherman relentlessly brought his army toward Atlanta, forcing Johnston to do the same.

Still, Sherman's need for supplies kept him close to the rail line running down from Chattanooga, Tennessee. The fast-riding, hard-hitting Confederate **cavalry** led by Major General Nathan Bedford Forrest frequently broke up the supply line. Annoyed, Sherman sent 8,000 troops after them. On June 10, at Brice's Crossroads, Mississippi, Forrest defeated the Union force, which was twice as large as his. A month later, about 14,000 Union soldiers fought Forrest at Tupelo, Mississippi. After taking heavy casualties, Forrest had to halt his raiding.

NATHAN BEDFORD FORREST

Nathan Bedford Forrest was a self-made man. Born into poverty in Kentucky in 1821, he built what he claimed was a $1.5-million fortune, a huge sum for the time. When the Civil War broke out, he used his own money to equip a cavalry troop.

Forrest perfected the art of the cavalry raid, attacking Union supply trains with great success. When his units were attached to larger armies, Forrest often quarreled with the commanding officers. He also developed a reputation for brutality, and his men were accused of killing black Union soldiers who had surrendered when he captured Fort Pillow, Tennessee, in 1864.

After the war, Forrest worked to rebuild his fortune. He also became a leader of the Ku Klux Klan, a secret organization that arose in the South to terrorize the recently freed slaves with whippings and lynchings. He died in 1877.

Falling Back

As the weeks wore on, Sherman continued south. There were occasional fights—at Resaca, Georgia, on May 14 and 15; at New Hope Church, Georgia, from May 25 to 28; at Kennesaw Mountain, Georgia, on June 27. By early July, Johnston's Confederate forces had been pushed back right to Atlanta.

Johnston had masterfully kept his army intact. He had not attacked, however, and his soldiers were growing dismayed.

So was Jefferson Davis, who had never favored a defensive strategy. Once Sherman reached the gates of Atlanta, Davis could not bear to leave Johnston in command. On July 17, he replaced him with a tough fighter from Lee's army, John Bell Hood. Believing that his job was to attack, attack Hood did—disastrously for the Confederacy.

Fighting Outside Atlanta

Wasting no time, Hood attacked at Peachtree Creek, north of the city, on July 20, 1864. The Confederates ran into the stout defenses of George Thomas and suffered heavy casualties, nearly forty-eight hundred men compared to Thomas's nearly eighteen hundred. Two days later, Hood attacked again, this time east of the city. Hood again suffered heavy losses, this time from seven thousand to ten thousand men compared to about thirty-

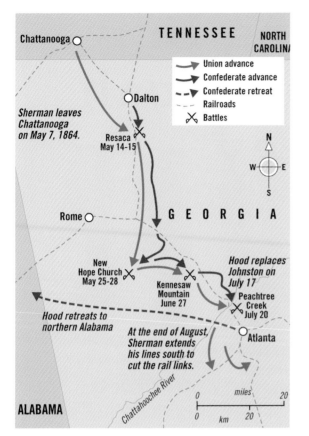

Johnston shadowed Sherman's army on its march south to Atlanta, hoping to find a favorable position to block his progress.

seven hundred for Sherman. Just six days later, on July 28, Hood attacked west of the city. In the Battle of Ezra Church, Hood lost perhaps as many as five thousand men compared to only six hundred or so Union soldiers.

Hood's attacks had bled his army—already outnumbered—of several thousand troops, but they had also checked Sherman's advance. Atlanta's defenses were strong, surrounding the city without a break; Sherman knew it would be folly for him to attack head-on. He opted for a siege.

JOHN BELL HOOD

*Born in Kentucky in 1831, John Bell Hood graduated from West Point—although he did not excel—in 1853. Serving on the frontier, he remained in the army until the Civil War broke out. He served in Lee's Army of Northern Virginia, where he commanded a regiment, then several regiments, and finally a **division**. At the battle of Gettysburg in 1863, he suffered a painful arm wound.*

In 1863, Hood and his division moved west with General James Longstreet. At Chickamauga, he was wounded in the leg, and it had to be amputated. He then became the commander of the Confederate Army of the Tennessee.

After the war, Hood settled in New Orleans and became a merchant. He died in a yellow fever epidemic in 1879.

CHAPTER FIVE

Fighting in the Shenandoah Valley

Assault on the Valley

While Sherman was advancing on Atlanta, Grant's army was pounding Lee's in several bloody battles in the area north of Richmond. Western Virginia, home to the Shenandoah Valley, saw more fighting. Flanked by the Blue Ridge Mountains on the east, the Appalachian Mountains on the west, and leading up to Maryland, Shenandoah Valley was the highway Lee had taken twice to invade the North. Crops from this fertile area helped feed his army. Grant wanted to control the Valley.

About 250 teenage cadets from nearby Virginia Military Institute (VMI) won fame in the South by taking part in the battle of New Market in 1864.

He sent General Franz Sigel and sixty-five hundred men, who were defeated by a smaller Confederate force at New Market on May 15, 1864. Grant replaced Sigel with General David Hunter, who was stopped when his troops ran into a portion of Robert E. Lee's Army of Northern Virginia commanded by General Jubal Early. Instead of going back into the Valley, however, Hunter crossed the Allegheny Mountains to West Virginia, which left the valley open to Early.

Early grabbed the opportunity. By July 6, 1864, his 15,000 soldiers were in Maryland. Turning east, they marched to Washington, D.C. Reaching the capital's suburbs, they burned and looted several homes. Grant quickly sent troops, and Early had to pull back, but his raid had scared many Northerners.

Burning the Valley

Grant next sent General Philip Sheridan and 40,000 troops after Jubal Early. On September 19, 1864, Sheridan attacked at Winchester, Virginia, and forced Early to retreat. Three days later, Sheridan attacked again near Strasburg and once more forced Early to fall back.

Early had one trick left, however. He sneaked up on Sheridan's army,

JUBAL EARLY

Born in Virginia in 1816, Jubal Early graduated from West Point in 1837 but served only one year in the army. After resigning, he became a lawyer and a state legislator. Early voted against leaving the Union at Virginia's secession convention. When the majority overruled him, he joined the Confederate army and fought in most of the battles of the Army of Northern Virginia, from First Bull Run in 1861 to Cold Harbor.

After the war, Early returned to practicing law. He also carried on a paper war in speeches and in the press with James Longstreet, who had written critically about some of Lee's decisions. Early rose to their old commander's defense and helped popularize the image of Lee as a hero of the South.

A PRESIDENT IN DANGER

On July 12, 1864, Early's troops fired on Union soldiers near Fort Stevens, where President Lincoln and his wife, Mary Todd Lincoln, were watching the battle. Seeing a tall civilian standing on the wall, one Union soldier shouted, "Get down, you . . . fool, before you get shot!" The civilian—President Lincoln—complied. The captain who gave that sound advice was Oliver Wendell Holmes Jr., later a justice of the U.S. Supreme Court.

PHILIP SHERIDAN

Born in New York City in 1831, Philip Sheridan began the war as a supply officer but was soon given a cavalry command. He fought in a number of battles in the West and gained several promotions. When Grant moved east, he took Sheridan with him to lead the cavalry of the Army of the Potomac.

After the war, Sheridan served for a while as military governor of Texas and Louisiana. When he ordered the governors of those states removed from office, he was relieved of the command. He succeeded Sherman and served as overall commander of the U.S. Army until his death in 1888.

Lieutenant General Grant
ordered General Sheridan to make

". . . the Shenandoah Valley a barren waste . . . so that crows flying over it for the balance of this season will have to carry their [food] with them."

Union divisions running to the rear. The hungry Confederates then fell upon the food the well-supplied Union army had left behind. That was their doom, as Sheridan then had time to organize a fierce counterattack that rolled over the Southerners. Early's army scattered, and Sheridan had mastery of the valley.

Grant wanted to make sure that the farms of the Shenandoah Valley could not be used to feed Lee's army. Sheridan carried out this work with a vengeance. His army burned food, barns, and homes, killing animals and destroying anything that could be used to support the Confederate army. Sheridan reported that his men had ". . . destroyed more than two thousand barns filled with wheat, hay, and farming implements." This destruction embittered many in the South.

which was camped at Cedar Creek. On October 19, Early's army attacked at dawn, sending four surprised

"Total War?"

Sheridan's destruction of the valley showed that Grant saw war in a new

General Philip Sheridan returned from a meeting in Washington, D.C., just in time to rally his troops at Cedar Creek, Virginia.

way. In the past, armies had aimed to capture capital cities or defeat opposing armies. However, the Civil War was fought in the industrial era, when countries raised mass armies that were supported by farms and factories. Historians debate whether Sheridan's actions—and those of Sherman in the deeper South—qualify as "total war" since destroying the country's ability to support an enemy's army became just as important as destroying the army. While General Philip Sheridan's and General William Sherman's actions do not compare to the massive attacks on civilians of World War II, the Northern destruction certainly hurt Southerners and signaled a change in the nature of war.

CHAPTER SIX

Lincoln Reelected

Before the presidential election, Confederate general
Robert E. Lee told General James Longstreet:

*"If we can break up the enemy's arrangements early, and throw
him back, he will not be able to recover his position or his morale
until the presidential election is over, and then we shall
have a new president to treat with."*

An Election Looms

The battles of 1864 determined more than the fate of armies. The North was to hold a presidential election in November of that year. The outcome would rest on whether Northerners wanted to continue fighting and would accept the end of slavery.

Army successes would ensure Abraham Lincoln's reelection, but Southerners were determined to deny the Union those successes. They believed that if Lincoln's opponent won the election, the new president would agree to a peace plan giving the South independence.

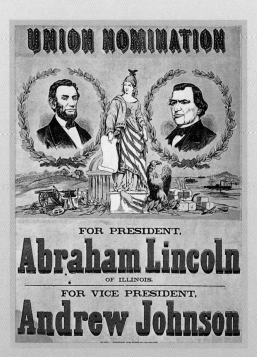

As his vice president on the Union ticket, Lincoln picked a Tennessee Democrat and Southern senator who supported the war, Andrew Johnson.

The Nominees

Though there was a brief challenge to him, Lincoln was nominated again by the Republicans on June 8, 1864. The Democrats chose Union general George Brinton McClellan. The language of the Democratic Party's **platform** hinted that his election would end the war, complaining about "four years of failure to restore the Union by the experiment of war." According to the platform, the war had trampled on the Constitution and the rights of citizens. It proposed to call for a convention of the states, where a peace agreement could be reached. Rejecting this idea, McClellan insisted he would continue the war but would fight only to restore the Union, not to end slavery.

In the summer of 1864, Lincoln seemed to be in trouble. The war had lasted much longer—and cost many more lives—than most people had expected. Democrats attacked sharply, pointing to horrific losses in Virginia and calling the new Union commander "butcher Grant."

Democratic presidential candidate George McClellan had commanded the Union army in the East from 1861 to 1862.

As August dragged on, a Democratic newspaper pointed to Sherman bogged down outside Atlanta, Georgia, and to Grant stuck outside Petersburg, Virginia, and asked, "Who shall revive the withered hopes that bloomed at the opening of Grant's **campaign**?" On top of that, Confederate general Early had almost reached the nation's capital.

Lincoln did not expect to win reelection. In late August, he wrote, "It seems exceedingly probable that this Administration will not be reelected."

After evacuating Atlanta, Hood ordered his ammunition trains destroyed; the wheels of the train cars littered the ground. The chimneys were once part of a factory, also destroyed by the fleeing Confederates.

In the states that counted soldiers' ballots separately, Lincoln won 78 percent of the votes compared to only 22 percent for McClellan.

The Tide of War—and the Election—Turns

September brought good news for Lincoln. On September 1, 1864, Confederate general John Hood was forced to evacuate Atlanta. The next day, Sherman's army moved in. A few weeks later, Union general Philip Sheridan scored successes against General Early in the Shenandoah Valley in Virginia. No longer did the president's war policy seem a failure.

In the end, Lincoln won, beating

A British correspondent said the Union soldiers' votes showed that Northerners

". . . are in earnest in a way the like of which the world never saw before, silently, calmly, but desperately in earnest."

George McClellan by more than 400,000 popular votes and winning a huge electoral vote majority —212 to 21. Soldiers helped him win. Their votes, counted sep-

Many in the South remained defiant, despite Lincoln's overwhelming victory, as Jefferson Davis showed in a message to the Confederate Congress late in 1864:

*"Nothing has changed in the purpose of [the Confederacy's] Government, in the **indomitable** valor of its troops, or in the unquenchable spirit of its people."*

arately in a number of states, show over-whelming support for Lincoln, a powerful expres-sion of the North's will to continue fighting for the Union—and for emancipation.

THE SECOND INAUGURAL ADDRESS

Lincoln's second inaugural address, given in March 1865, reflected his thinking about the war. He continued to blame the war on the South, saying it had preferred to "make war rather than let [the United States] survive." He stated that the chief cause of the war was slavery. He suggested that the huge human cost of the war was the price the nation had to pay to make up for the sin of slavery.

Finally, Lincoln looked forward to the North and South becoming reconciled and living together in peace. He cautioned Northerners not to be arrogant in victory: "With malice toward none, with charity for all, with firmness in the right as God gives us to see the right, let us strive on to finish the work we are in, to bind up the nation's wounds . . . to do all which may achieve and cherish a just and lasting peace among ourselves and with all nations."

One of the thousands of spectators at Lincoln's second inaugural was John Wilkes Booth, his future assassin.

CHAPTER SEVEN

Sherman's March to the Sea

General Sherman was a determined and aggressive fighter, like his friend Ulysses S. Grant. In early 1865, however, he offered generous surrender terms to a Confederate army.

Sherman's Plan

Union general Sherman had met one of his objectives in taking Atlanta, but Hood's army was still alive and kicking, and Forrest's cavalry was once again nipping at his supply line. Hood hoped to force Sherman to abandon Atlanta by moving his 40,000-man army north into Tennessee, but Sherman had other ideas.

Sherman wanted to leave Union general George Thomas and 60,000 men in Tennessee to deal with Hood and Forrest. He would take another 60,000 and march from Atlanta to the Atlantic Ocean. His army would ignore supply lines and live off the land, a risky move. Sherman pointed out the advantages of this move to Grant:

"If we can march a well-appointed army right through [Confederate] territory, it is a demonstration to the world, foreign and domestic, that we have a power which Davis cannot resist."

In the meantime, Sherman outraged many in the South by ordering all civilians to leave Atlanta. He was accused of being inhumane, a charge he dismissed as hypocritical. His army could not care for the women, children, and old people, he said. He argued that they would be better off in "places of safety among their own friends." Still, Sherman's order was as much punishment to Atlanta as it was concern for the people's welfare.

Grant and Lincoln, though reluctant at first, agreed to Sherman's plan. On November 16, 1864, Sherman's army set out. It remained out of touch with other Northern armies throughout the march. Sherman told Grant to read Richmond's newspapers to follow his progress.

Franklin and Nashville

Hood still hoped to force Sherman to abandon Atlanta by moving north. Thomas's army was split, and Hood hoped to defeat the pieces of that Union army separately. On November 30, he threw his forces at about 27,000 Northerners at Franklin, Tennessee, just south of Nashville. Though they managed to break through, the Union army held a new line against further attacks. Hood lost more than double the Union casualties in the fierce fighting.

Six Confederate generals were killed in the battle, with five more wounded and one captured. More poignant, perhaps, was the fate of Confederate captain Tod Carter. Wounded, he crawled to the porch of his nearby family home, where his family discovered him the next morning, dead.

The Union troops fell back to Nashville, where they joined the rest of Thomas's army. Hood followed. On December 15, Thomas attacked Hood. Thomas's troops pushed the Confederates out of their defenses on the first day of fighting. Attacks the next day completely overran Hood's soldiers.

In the two days of fighting at Nashville, Hood lost about 6,000 troops. Of that total, 4,500 had been captured by the fast-moving Northern attack. Hood's army was broken. When it gathered in Tupelo, Mississippi, a few weeks later, little more than 20,000 soldiers could be assembled. Some days later, Hood resigned his command.

The March to the Sea

While Hood's army was being devastated, Sherman's was marching 285 miles (460 km) to Savannah, Georgia.

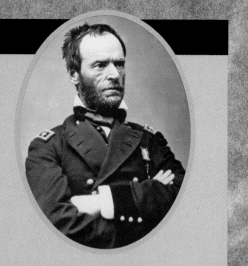

WILLIAM
TECUMSEH SHERMAN

William Tecumseh Sherman, born in Ohio in 1820, graduated from West Point and served in the Mexican War (1846–1848). He resigned from the army and, after failing in other ventures, became the head of a Louisiana military school. After secession, Sherman reluctantly returned to the North— he liked Southerners.

Sherman's sound command at Shiloh gained him a promotion, and he became Grant's right-hand man. He drew criticism in the South for the destruction his army inflicted on the march to the Atlantic Ocean. During the march itself, however, Sherman told Southerners that once the war ended, his army would give them food; "I will share with you my last cracker." After the war, Sherman served as the overall commander of the army. He died in 1891.

For the Northern soldiers, opposed by only a few thousand cavalry troops, it was a picnic.

For Southerners, it was a catastrophe. Sherman told his men to take all the food they needed. As Sheridan had done in the Shenandoah Valley, he wanted to take or destroy all the South's food so that it could no longer be used by Southern armies. His "bummers," as the **foragers** were called, caused a great deal of damage. One of Sherman's officers explained the reasoning: "Nothing can end this war but some demonstration of [Southerners'] helplessness."

In mid-December 1864, Sherman reached the outskirts of Savannah. A small force of ten thousand Confederates abandoned the city on December 20, and two days later, Sherman's men marched in. A government worker in Richmond wrote, "Men are silent, and some dejected. It is unquestionably the darkest period we have yet experienced."

When William Tecumseh Sherman entered Savannah, Georgia, he sent a telegram to President Lincoln:

"I beg to present to you, as a Christmas gift, the city of Savannah, with 150 heavy guns and plenty of ammunition, and also about 25,000 bales of cotton."

As Sherman's army advanced to the sea, it was joined by thousands of African Americans marching their own way to freedom.

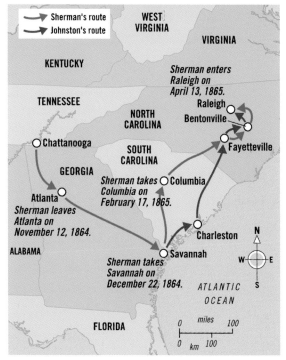

Sherman's army needed little more than a month to cross the nearly 300 miles (460 km) from Atlanta to Savannah. They met little opposition on the entire route.

Turning North

On February 1, 1865, Sherman turned his army north, heading to South Carolina. To many Northern soldiers, South Carolina—the first state to secede from the Union—had caused the Civil War. As one soldier declared, "Here is where treason began and, by God, here is where it shall end!" Sherman's army did far more damage there than it had in Georgia. Soldiers not only destroyed crops, they even burned houses— which they stopped doing when they reached North Carolina.

The End

~

In March 1865, Lincoln met with generals Sherman (left) and Grant (second from left) and Admiral David Dixon Porter (right) to discuss final war plans and ways to deal with the surrender of Confederate armies.

Gloomy Prospects

In the winter of 1864 to 1865, the Confederacy was faltering. Spirits were low due to Hood's defeats, Sherman's march, and Lee's inability to break out of Petersburg. On top of that, the Confederate army was melting away. By late 1864, Richmond records said that the South had just over 400,000 soldiers. Of that total, only 196,000 were counted as present and ready for duty. That is, nearly half of the Confederacy's fighting force had deserted—left the army and gone home. Badly weakened Confederate armies were growing less able to resist continuing Union advances.

Desperate Southern leaders began discussing the idea of bringing slaves into the army to do routine camp chores, such as cooking and caring for animals. This would allow the white soldiers doing those jobs to join the fighting ranks. In

March of 1865, in one of the last acts of the Confederate Congress, it finally passed a law allowing slaves to enlist in the army. The law came too late to have any real effect, however.

Meeting of the Minds

Despite the growing problems, Confederate president Jefferson Davis remained determined to win. Some Confederate leaders suggested calling for a peace conference. Davis sent Vice President Alexander Stephens and two others to meet with Lincoln. They were instructed, however, only to negotiate for peace between "two countries," not to rejoin the Union.

They met on February 3, 1865, with President Lincoln and Secretary of State William Seward, but the meeting was fruitless. Lincoln insisted that peace could only come when the South agreed to return to the Union and accept the end of slavery. The Southerners would not accept those terms.

Trouble at Petersburg

Meanwhile, as the siege of Petersburg dragged on, Lee's army was in serious trouble. During the fall of 1864, Grant had tried to move around the sides of Lee's trenches. Lee had countered by extending his lines. Eventually, his 60,000 or so men were stretched along lines 35 miles

(55 km) long—far too long for his men to adequately defend.

Worse, his men were hungry. Every day, more than one hundred boats and another one hundred barges brought supplies to Grant's 110,000 soldiers. Lee's army, on the other hand, had only a few days' rations at a time.

A New Role and a New Plan

On February 6, 1865, Lee assumed the new post of commander of all Confederate armies. Soon after, he brought Joseph Johnston back to patch together a defense against Sherman. Then he developed a last, desperate plan; he would send some of his army to join with Johnston and beat Sherman. This combined Confederate force would then return to Petersburg and defeat Grant.

To carry out his plan, Lee needed to make a hole in Grant's lines. He hoped that Grant would then consolidate his forces so that he could shorten his own lines. Only then could he afford to send part of his army away. Attacking before dawn on March 25, his troops overran a defensive point called Fort Stedman. They pressed on, but a strong Union counterattack overwhelmed them. The Southerners retreated to their own lines, leaving four thousand casualties behind, many of them prisoners.

The defeat at Five Forks was a terrible blow to the Confederacy. Nearly half of the ten thousand Southern soldiers there surrendered.

Five Forks

Meanwhile, Johnston had also met a similar defeat at Bentonville, North Carolina. While the Confederate attack was successful early in the battle, a powerful Union counterattack defeated the Southerners. Johnston was forced to fall back.

Toward the end of March, Grant began to move his army south and west of Lee's to cut off any chance that Lee would join Johnston. Sheridan brought a strong force to a vital crossroads named Five Forks, Virginia, where he overcame General George Pickett's Confederates. Grant then ordered an attack on April 2, 1865, all along the weakened Petersburg lines. Here, too, the Northern troops overran the defenses.

Richmond Falls

Lee sent word to Jefferson Davis that he had to abandon his lines and warned that the Confederate government should abandon Richmond. Davis and most of the remainder of the Confederate government left town that day. The next day, the Union army marched into the Confederate capital. A Richmond woman wrote, "I saw them unfurl a tiny flag, and I sank on my knees, and the bitter, bitter tears came in a torrent."

As Confederate government officials flee the city, Richmond erupts in fires set by retreating soldiers attempting to destroy supplies they could not carry.

Final Days

Lee pulled out of Petersburg on April 2 and marched west, hoping to find some expected supplies. The Union army was in hot pursuit. At Sayler's Creek, Virginia, Lee's army was split, and one section came under attack. Nearly eight thousand Confederate soldiers surrendered; Lee's army was now a fraction of its former strength.

Lee realized that he could not continue. On April 9, 1865, he met with Grant in Appomattox Court House, Virginia. Lee wore his best dress uniform, while Grant had on the dirty private's field jacket he always wore. They signed a paper in which

CONTINUING WAR BY STEALTH

In the waning months and weeks of the Confederacy, many Southerners thought about continuing to fight. By fighting a **guerrilla war***—breaking the armies up into small units—they could harass Union soldiers. Some even thought they could keep the Confederacy alive in this way.*

Lee believed a guerrilla war would be very destructive. Soldiers would become thieves who had to steal to feed themselves, and Union armies would move even deeper into the South, seeking out the guerrillas and destroying even more farms and homes. Lee also believed that such a strategy could not succeed.

Wilmer McLean's home in Appomattox saw a climactic scene of the war.

TRYING TO ESCAPE THE WAR

In 1861 and 1862, Virginian Wilmer McLean was dismayed to see two armies fight twice on his farm near Manassas Junction. Determined to move out of danger, he sold the land and bought a house in the village of Appomattox Court House, far west of Richmond. The war, however, found McLean once again. It was in his house that Lee surrendered to Grant.

Lee surrendered his army. Informed that Lee's army had no food, Grant agreed to send them spare rations.

Three days later, Robert E. Lee's army formally gave up its battle flags and weapons. John Gordon led the first units to reach the Union soldiers. A Northern officer ordered his men to salute the Confederate general, who ordered his men to do the same in return. In this way, at their last meeting, the two armies that had fought so bitterly for so long paid tribute to each other.

In the 1960s, artist Thomas Lovell painted this picture of Lee's surrender to Grant. Lee is at the table on the left side of the painting

Reaction

News of Lee's surrender spread like wildfire. In the South, many agreed with Sarah Morgan, who wrote in her diary, "All things are taken from us, and become portions and parcels of the dreadful past." Across the North, people celebrated. A reporter described the scene in Washington, D.C.: "Almost by magic the streets were crowded with hosts of people, talking, laughing, hurrahing, and shouting in the fullness of their joy."

Other Confederate armies followed Lee's example. On April 26, General Joseph Johnston surrendered to Sherman. On May 4, the Confederate forces in Alabama, Mississippi, and Louisiana surrendered. Little more than three weeks later, on May 26, the last major Confederate army—the one west of the Mississippi River—gave up.

On May 10, 1865, Union soldiers on horseback caught up with the fleeing Jefferson Davis. They captured the Confederate president, his wife, some aides, and their army escort. Davis spent the next two years in prison.

A Night at the Theater

Before the last surrenders, one more tragic death punctuated the long, bloody war. It came on Friday, April 14, 1865—the same day, ironically, that the U.S. flag was raised once again over Fort Sumter.

That very night, Abraham Lincoln and his wife went to see a comedy at Washington's Ford's Theater. During the play, Confederate sympathizer John Wilkes Booth sneaked into the box where the president sat, pointed a pistol at the back of Lincoln's head, and fired. Leaping down to the stage—and breaking his leg in the process—Booth escaped.

Lincoln's face shows the wear of four years of war. This photograph was taken just four days before he was assassinated.

Lincoln was carried to a room across the street. He died the following morning.

The tragic news stunned people on both sides. Northerner Sidney George Fisher wrote that Lincoln's death "is a terrible loss to the country, perhaps an even greater

THE CONSPIRATORS

Eight others were tried and found guilty of helping Booth. Edman Spangler was sentenced to six years in prison for helping Booth escape. Samuel Arnold and Michael O'Laughlen were each sentenced to life in prison for joining Booth in a plan to kidnap Lincoln, as was Dr. Samuel Mudd, who had treated Booth's broken leg. Mudd and Arnold were later paroled. O'Laughlen died of yellow fever in prison.

Four others were sentenced to death and hanged. Accompanied by David Herold, Lewis Powell had stabbed Secretary of State William Seward the same night that Lincoln was shot. George Atzerodt was supposed to kill Vice President Andrew Johnson, although he did not attempt it. Mary Surratt ran the boardinghouse where Booth lived and, according to one witness, knew of the conspiracy. Many now believe she was innocent.

Surratt's son John escaped to Canada. He was later captured and tried, but he was released when the jury could not reach a verdict. John Surratt, who maintained that he had nothing to do with killing Lincoln, lived until 1916.

Lincoln and his wife were sitting in this box at Ford's Theater when Booth shot him.

JOHN WILKES BOOTH

John Wilkes Booth was born in Bel Air, Maryland, in 1838. Like his older brother Edwin, Booth followed his father, Junius Brutus Booth, and became an actor. John Wilkes Booth was a strong Confederate sympathizer and hated Lincoln. He initially planned to kidnap Lincoln and bring him to Richmond so he could be exchanged for Confederate prisoners of war. When that plot failed, Booth decided to kill the president.

On April 26, 1865, a cavalry troop tracked Booth down, cornering him in a barn in northern Virginia. He was shot and died a few hours later.

loss to the South than to the North, for Mr. Lincoln's humanity [and] kindness of heart stood between them and the [Republicans] who urge measures of vengeance." Many Southerners feared that they would be blamed for Lincoln's death.

Amid the shock and grief, Vice President Andrew Johnson was sworn in as president. Funeral services were held for Lincoln on April 19 in Washington. Then, his body was put on a train that carried it across the North—to many tearful tributes—to be buried in Springfield, Illinois. Lincoln's death gave a final conclusion to the four long, bloody, destructive years of war.

1863 *July 1–3:* Union victory at Gettysburg ends Robert E. Lee's last invasion of North.

July 3: Confederates at Vicksburg, Mississippi, surrender.

July 9: Confederates at Port Hudson, Louisiana, surrender, giving Union control of the Mississippi River.

Sep. 9: Confederates abandon Chattanooga, Tennessee, giving Union an important crossroads.

Sep. 19–20: Confederate victory at Chickamauga, Georgia.

Nov. 23–25: Union victory at Chattanooga secures Tennessee.

1864 *Mar. 10:* Ulysses S. Grant is named as commander of all Union armies.

May 5–6: Battle of the Wilderness, Virginia, produces high casualties for Union and Confederates.

May 7: General William Sherman's army leaves Chattanooga for Atlanta, Georgia.

May 8–19: More high casualties at battle of Spotsylvania, Virginia.

May 12: Early's raid reaches Washington, D.C., scaring Union government.

May 14–15: Sherman and Confederate general Joseph Johnston clash at Resaca, Georgia; Sherman's advance to Atlanta continues.

May 15: Confederate victory at New Market, Virginia, threatens Union control of Shenandoah Valley.

June 1–3: Lee stops Union attack once more at battle of Cold Harbor, Virginia.

June 18: Siege begins at Petersburg, Virginia.

June 27: Sherman and Johnston fight at Kennesaw Mountain, Georgia.

July 14: Battle of Tupelo, Mississippi, forces Forrest to end raiding.

July 17: Hood replaces Johnston as commander of Army of the Tennessee.

July 20: Union victory at battle of Peachtree Creek, Georgia, weakens Hood's army with heavy casualties.

July 22: Union victory at battle of Atlanta.

July 30: Union forces fail to end siege of Petersburg at Battle of the Crater.

Aug. 31: Democrats nominate General George McClellan for president.

Sep. 2: Union army moves into Atlanta.

Oct. 19: Union victory at Cedar Creek gives Union control of Shenandoah Valley.

Nov. 16: Sherman's army begins march to the sea, aimed at showing Northern power, Southern weakness.

Dec. 15–16: Union victory at Nashville, Tennessee, ends last desperate Southern invasion.

Dec. 22: Sherman takes Savannah, Georgia, reaching Atlantic Ocean.

1865 *Feb. 3:* Lincoln and Confederate officials meet for peace conference, which fails.

Feb. 6: Lee is given command of all Confederate troops.

Mar. 19–21: Sherman continues advance with victory at Bentonville, North Carolina.

Mar. 25: Confederate attack at Fort Stedman, Virginia, fails.

Apr. 1: Union victory at Five Forks, Virginia, threatens survival of Lee's army.

Apr. 2: Lee abandons lines at Petersburg; Confederate government abandons Richmond.

Apr. 9: Lee surrenders to Grant.

Apr. 14: John Wilkes Booth kills Lincoln.

Apr. 26: Johnston surrenders to Sherman at Durham Station, North Carolina; Booth killed.

May 10: Jefferson Davis captured; President Johnson declares the end of war.

May 26: Last major Confederate army surrenders.

artillery: large, heavy weapons such as cannons; also used to refer to the branch of the army that uses such weapons.

Border States: the states on the northern edge of the southern states, where there was slavery, but it was not a very strong part of society; includes Delaware, Maryland, Kentucky, and Missouri. After bitter and sometimes bloody struggles, these four states remained with the Union.

breastworks: defenses made of wood that soldiers could hide behind while firing on an attacking force.

campaign: a series of army movements aimed at achieving a particular objective.

casualties: the people killed, wounded, captured, and missing in a battle.

cavalry: soldiers fighting on horseback.

Confederacy: also called "the South;" another name for the Confederate States of America, the nation formed by the states that had seceded—Virginia, Tennessee, North Carolina, South Carolina, Georgia, Alabama, Mississippi, Louisiana, Texas, Arkansas, and Florida.

contrabands: property of an enemy that an army seizes.

corps: an army unit that includes two to four divisions, consisting of about 20,000 to 30,000 troops.

division: an army unit that included from about ten to fifteen regiments and totaled about ten thousand soldiers.

foragers: soldiers who gather food for an army from the wild or from the produce of the countryside they are crossing.

guerrilla war: attacks on an opposing army by small bands of fighters who are not part of a regular army and who strike quickly by surprise and then escape.

indomitable: unable to be overcome.

infantry: soldiers that fight on foot.

platform: a political party's statement of its plans if it should win an election.

regiments: units of soldiers that included ten companies of one hundred soldiers each.

reinforcements: soldiers added to a force.

reserves: troops initially held out of a battle so a commander can use them to add to an attack or reinforce defenders.

secede: to leave the Union.

siege: surrounding and bombarding a fortified position with artillery, preventing food or supplies from reaching the enemy.

Union: also called "the North;" another name for the United States of America, which, after the secession of Southern states, included Maine, Vermont, New Hampshire, Massachusetts, Rhode Island, Connecticut, New York, New Jersey, Pennsylvania, Delaware, Maryland, Ohio, Michigan, Indiana, Illinois, Kentucky, Wisconsin, Minnesota, Iowa, Kansas, Missouri, Oregon, and California; in 1863, West Virginia seceded from Virginia and entered the Union as a separate state.

West Point: the United States Military Academy, located in West Point, New York, where cadets are trained in military arts.

Further Resources

These web sites and books cover the last years of the war:

WEBSITES

www.civilwaralbum.com The Civil War Album includes modern and wartime photos of Civil War sites and maps.

www.civilwarhome.com Follow links on this Civil War enthusiast's homepage to essays on civil war battles, biographies, letters to and from soldiers, and information on a variety of topics.

www.nps.gov/apco The National Park Service's web site for the Appomattox Court House.

www.nps.gov/chch The Chickamauga and Chattanooga National Military Park web sites.

www.nps.gov/frsp The Fredericksburg and Spotsylvania National Military Park web site provides information about "the bloodiest landscape in North America," and includes detailed information on soldiers and battles.

www.nps.gov/pete/mahan/kidspageintro. html Petersburg National Battlefield web site.

www.pbs.org/wgbh/amex/lincolns Covers politics, slavery, and more.

BOOKS

Gregson, Susan R. *Ulysses S. Grant* (Let Freedom Ring: Civil War Biographies). Mankato, MN: Bridgestone Books, 2002.

Groom, Winston. *Shrouds of Glory: From Atlanta to Nashville.* New York: Atlantic Monthly Press, 1995.

Kerby, Mona. *Robert E. Lee: Southern Hero of the Civil War.* Springfield, N.J.: Enslow, 1997.

King, David C. *Ulysses S. Grant* (Triangle Histories—The Civil War). Woodbridge, CN: Blackbirch Marketing, 2001.

Marinelli, Deborah A. *The Assassination of Abraham Lincoln* (Library of Political Assassinations). New York: Rosen, 2002.

Remstein, Henna. *William Sherman: Union General* (Famous Figures of the Civil War Era) Philadelphia: Chelsea House, 2001.

Yancey, Diane. *Leaders of the North and South* (American War Library). San Diego: Lucent Books, 2000.

Index

Page numbers in *italics* indicate maps and diagrams.

Math Counts

Length

Children's Press®
An Imprint of Scholastic Inc.

About This Series

In keeping with the major goals of the National Council of Teachers of Mathematics, children will become mathematical problem solvers, learn to communicate mathematically, and learn to reason mathematically by using the series Math Counts.

Pattern, Shape, and *Size* may be investigated first—in any sequence.

Sorting, Counting, and *Numbers* may be used next, followed by *Time, Length, Weight,* and *Capacity.*

—Ramona G. Choos, Professor of Mathematics,
Senior Adviser to the Dean of Continuing Education, Chicago State University;
Sponsor for Chicago Elementary Teachers' Mathematics Club

Author's Note

Mathematics is a part of a child's world. It is not only interpreting numbers or mastering tricks of addition or multiplication. Mathematics is about ideas. These ideas have been developed to explain particular qualities such as size, weight, and height, as well as relationships and comparisons. Yet all too often the important part that an understanding of mathematics will play in a child's development is forgotten or ignored.

Most adults can solve simple mathematical tasks without the need for counters, beads, or fingers. Young children find such abstractions almost impossible to master. They need to see, talk, touch, and experiment.

The photographs and text in these books have been chosen to encourage talk about topics that are essentially mathematical. By talking, the young reader can explore some of the central concepts that support mathematics. It is on an understanding of these concepts that a student's future mastery of mathematics will be built.

—Henry Pluckrose

Math Counts

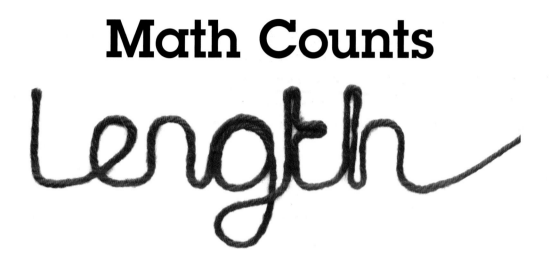

By Henry Pluckrose

Mathematics Consultant: Ramona G. Choos, Professor of Mathematics

Children's Press®

An Imprint of Scholastic Inc.

How long is the string in this ball?

How long is this truck? Sometimes we need to measure things to find out exactly how long they are.

We use the word *length* to describe the measurement of something from one end to the other. We talk about the length of a swimming pool,

the length of a race,

the length of a highway,

8

or a length of fabric.

You could measure the length
of a table by counting in hand spans,

but people's hands are not all the same size.

You could measure
the length of a lawn
by counting paces,

but people's
paces are not all
the same size.

If we want to measure exactly, we have to use a standard measure. Standard measures are the same everywhere. A surveyor measures the ground with a tape. The tape is divided into feet and inches or meters and centimeters.

It is important to be able to measure exactly. Architects draw detailed plans for builders to use. They have to make sure a building will fit on its space.

A tailor uses exact measurements. Short lengths are measured in inches or centimeters. Thirty-six inches make one yard. One hundred centimeters make one meter.

Scientists often study very small creatures. Tiny things are measured in fractions of an inch or in millimeters. Ten millimeters make one centimeter, about one-third of an inch.

Yards and inches are useful for measuring things that are not too long. In some countries, distances between places are measured in miles. One mile equals 1,760 yards.

PROSPECT PARK ZOO
3.7 MILES

BOROUGH HALL
2.7 MILES

GRACIE MANSION
11.4 MILES

CONEY ISLAND
11.4 MILES

PANAMA CANAL
2218

PEORIA, IL
932 MILES

MASIAKA 20 Km

KAMBIA 103 Km

KABALA 241 Km

BO 186 Km

In many other countries, a different standard measure is used to show distances between places. This sign shows distances in kilometers. One thousand meters make one kilometer. A mile is longer than a kilometer.

We also use feet and inches, or meters and centimeters, to measure height. The height of a person is measured from the soles of the feet to the top of the head. What is your height?

As you grow you become taller. Years ago, these basketball players were exactly the same height as you are today. How do you know?

We use the word *height* to describe many other things. The height of a building is measured from the ground to the very top.

The height of this cliff is measured from the level of the sea to the grassy land at the top.

Mountains also are measured from sea level. The peak, or top, of Mount Everest is 29,029 feet (8,848 meters) above sea level. Why is sea level used when giving the height of a mountain?

Aircraft pilots also measure the height at which their planes are flying.

We can describe the
height of things around
us by comparing them
with the height of our own
bodies. These plants have
not grown very tall,

but they seem enormous
to an earthworm.

These trees are very tall.
Their topmost branches
are far above the ground.

When trees are cut down for timber, a lumberjack measures the length of each trunk, not its height.

What is the difference between length

and height?

Index

Reader's Guide

Visit this Scholastic Web site to download the Reader's Guide for this series:
www.factsfornow.scholastic.com Enter the keywords **Math Counts**

Library of Congress Cataloging-in-Publication Data

Names: Pluckrose, Henry, 1931- author. | Choos, Ramona G.
Title: Length/by Henry Pluckrose; mathematics consultant, Ramona G. Choos, Professor of Mathematics.
Other titles: Math counts.
Description: Updated edition. | New York, NY: Children's Press, an imprint of Scholastic Inc., 2019. | Series: Math counts | Includes index.
Identifiers: LCCN 2017061278| ISBN 9780531175088 (library binding) | ISBN 9780531135174 (pbk.)
Subjects: LCSH: Length measurement—Juvenile literature.
Classification: LCC QC102 .P58 2019 | DDC 530.8—dc23
LC record available at https://lccn.loc.gov/2017061278

Copyright © The Watts Publishing Group, 2018
Printed in Heshan, China 62

Scholastic Inc., 557 Broadway, New York, NY 10012.

1 2 3 4 5 6 7 8 9 10 R 28 27 26 25 24 23 22 21 20 19

Photos ©: cover top: Serjio74/iStockphoto; cover bottom: Roni Mocan; 1: Roni Mocan; 3: Roni Mocan; 4: fotyma/iStockphoto; 5: 3dmentat/iStockphoto; 6: Paolo Bona/Shutterstock; 7: Chris Smith/Popperfoto/Getty Images; 8: kbwills/iStockphoto; 9: picturegarden/Getty Images; 10-11: Jenna Addesso; 12-13: Joshua Moise; 14: Photographee.eu/Fotolia; 15: Education Images/Getty Images; 16: Maskot/Getty Images; 17: Serjio74/iStockphoto; 18: Randy Duchaine/Alamy Images; 19: lcoccia/iStockphoto; 20: Redlink Production/age fotostock; 21: FatCamera/iStockphoto; 22: EllenMoran/iStockphoto; 23: prestongeorge/iStockphoto; 24: Zzvet/iStockphoto; 25: Artpilot/iStockphoto; 26: Jupiterimages/Getty Images; 27: shaunl/iStockphoto; 28: Serjio74/iStockphoto; 29: Lena Ason/Alamy Images; 30: FangXiaNuo/iStockphoto; 31: Michael Dodge/Getty Images.